pungent dins concentric

(Vanessa Couto Johnson)

Tolsun Books

Tolleson, Arizona

pungent dins concentric

Edited by Brandi Pischke

Cover art and design by David Pischke
Set in Adobe Caslon Pro, 11pt font. Design by Brandi Pischke

ISBN 978-1-948800-06-8

Published by Tolsun Books, LLC
Tolleson, Arizona
www.tolsunbooks.com

Acknowledgments

I offer thanks to the editors of these journals in which the following poems were taken in:

Blackbird, "c(on)ta(in)er" and "o(vers)ight"
Really System, "(t)ravel" and "neces(sit)ies"
Star 82 Review, "(trig)ger"
Storm Cellar, "en(try)," "k(itch)en," "(sw)um," and "anon"
Word Riot, "impen(ding)"
Vector, "ver(bat)im," "d(inner part)y," "bildungsroman," and "di(splay)"
Toad Suck Review, "longhand," "sidereal," "un(hi)de," "canoidea," "rot(is)erie,"
"leg(end)," "(sp)rang," and "dis(posit)ion"
MadHat Lit, "rebus"
Posit, "cyclor(am)a," "salu(brity)," "(sea)rch," and "v(as)cular"
The Destroyer, "case," "foo(t)no(t)e," "peri(met)er," "affix," and "concoct"
decomP magazine, "(even)ing"
Qwerty, "(a)ware" and "sp(ice)"
BORT Quarterly, "corr(elation)" and "(di)late"
Deluge, "cor(dial)," "ap(pet)ence," and "queue"
Two Serious Ladies, "birr," "hypnagoid," "megacosm"
baldhip, "reeling"
cream city review, "victual"
smoking glue gun, "g(at)her" and "(mime)sis"

Thanks to Susan Lewis of Posit for nominating "(sea)rch" for a Pushcart Prize.

Thank you, Samuel; my parents, your parents;
my friends, my colleagues; our atoms, our constellations.

Table of contents

Figure 1: Stimulus

Figure 2: The necessity of time for sound

Figure 3: For a common center, shape

pungent dins concentric

(Vanessa Couto Johnson)

Figure 1: Stimulus

(t)ravel

Intentions pave the road, but I clatter within a pothole. The bellybutton connoisseur scratches a new portal. Remote and screened, your laundry is lent. We borrow enough tire to go.

Water well enough to buck and does until dawn. Handles echo in my hands.

Plaid is a plain of perpendicular grass. Obtuse geese fan the sky.

The honk hunk between your hands in the metal animal, alloy ally of migration. Three-hundred-sixty degrees of antlers is too hot. GPS the melting point. Position the hood while riding in weather that is a constant.

Let t be the option I take as the second given. Clocks populate the apartment and I can hear them digesting. If your lizard breeds her eggs will have numbers.

neces(sit)ies

You tell me how the excrement of owls is oral. You blink slowly and your eyes rephrase themselves.

Mosquitoes hum in your living room until I tell you. You shut the door as I pin one in hand. We don't let them eat.

I make my leg acute on a chair at the café, asking if this is your method for double knots. One adult touching another adult's shoelaces, the turn and turn and enter. Shoe stay.

Soups or solids. Salads with goat cheese hoofsteps. My lactiferous ducts near the plate.

Whatever I am, you trace me, testing the cartilage of my nose with a press. We refuse stencils. We say that will be all.

Fry-piles make a half-moon on your plate while you continue a life of starch and iron. Those things I take off of you. One by one button. Meet and potato.

(sw)um

When you walk into the cold pool your face looks like it took a bad taste. I wait with dead bug surface tension at 4 ft.

My dark long hair infests your rugs. Egg-drop soup crossing the placemats.

Later, pandas on appropriated tables in a Mexican restaurant. If bamboo were onomatopoeia.

When you hear me, think of the phonetics of hunger. Shake crickets from a box for an orange fat-tailed cold blood.

We polylingual spoon nutrients, crave and carve and cave of deepening morphemes. You paint an inside without representation. Presentation. The climate ax swoosh, but I regain my temperature.

The real trees bark outside the window, but for now one language is enough.

anon

A mathematician parallel parks. 6ᵗʰ Street in Austin with buildings non-rhombohedral. Hipsters move like original chess pieces in the hand of an unknown Romanian.

Fail at alphabetizing because order is arbitrary. Mere memory, a vintage bought cheap in Kindergarten. We all speak English with the accent.

The accidental listener winds the box to hear the ticks again. Cog of mouth. We both habitually have hum spurts.

A cinema is showing *Aliens*. I strain my face between my fingers. This is my first viewing. I laugh my fear and fear my laugh in an audience. My sound a butter on the seat.

Recurring sets of thorax to thorax. Whisper lymphatic. Is everyone else really *that* boring. Am I no *common* denominator.

Every reptile needs its cave. We use one pillow. Fat as an algebraic letter. I do the same thing to both sides of the sign.

(prop)hyl(act)ic

Wisdom is not contagious. The genuine arches its back, rubbed.

Each word only describes the neurochemical park the trunks open in. Nails stutter in splintering hair.

The range of a face expressed in miles per hour. One foot removes another foot's toe-socks. We name a new unit to show efficiency. Working from base to given, logarithms in heat in winter.

You press against my data sets. I scan your health's diagonal, labeling it with a French letter.

A jet of adjectives because we refuse to enumerate only in verbs. Students could sting their calculators trying to catch.

Many theories with proper nouns on their coats, hoods up. They wear signs on their sleeves by wiping their noses.

Weather. Inside, outside. Repeat with me. Your jacket eventually thrown to the floor.

en(try)

A key inside your front door's lock withholds a knock-knock joke
or Houdini mind-trick. I interrupt its ambition with a force, hello.

Opposite, an ajar sliding glass patio door, wind flooding an august
chamber. Most of the day. Birds mock Pollock on your car.
Become driven, Jedi cognition of the father, who art.

I'm not interested in the word according to Luke. No illiciting on
my star step. Incant be.

All chili dogs go to heaven, that mouth I bliss. An opinion, then
Did you know that? An ion walks into a bar and orders a catatonic.

Karaoke, name that tunic. I put a lace on anything that is your
favorite.

Electoral volt. Benjamin Franklin my dear I don't give a Hoover
dam. But I do draw from the grid.

Unlike Houdini, you survive your appendicitis. Your organ
emigrates, leaving behind one wordless line.

k(itch)en

One out of four legs break. This is not a statistic but a moment of
your kitchen chair. I am sitting in its partner as you are cracked to
nadir, seated as startled as a hatchling.

A friend once thought you give chickens milk. Shake chocolate.
Carrot at the end of a stick or cherry at the end of a stem.

I pluck away buns, fork and knife double meat. Pickle wisps cheese
tar glittered lettuce. Mayonnaise be merry and bright.

You frown at any vinegar, but I've tablespooned. Balled chocolate
over roasted Brazil nuts.

You fail at correcting a kitten that claws two of your forearms. The
mammal sits behind you for a photo. Those ears polygon wild
appearing at your headtop. German on the mount, Liebling.

The three-legged chair stands, unnatural. A rugged pirate gone
redundant with pegged limbs. Cook what grows in the eye patch.

d(inner part)y

You sit as clear as a hologram across from me, our eyes nibbling. A fuss over your height, a grandmother quips you might be sitting on a bible. Unseen unknown.

There is always something on my facetious. Glutei maximi say no grace.

And this is not the mess of a garrison. Retired veterinarians approach a tank of fish they never serviced. Gumbo served; two occupants order.

Somewhere, a student spells *protestants* when she means *protestors*. This is not a country but citizens eating at three pushed tables. Colon colony of semicircle after semilunar.

Sniff night's last crescent. I would pull your smiles to my chin. But we are unattested to these witnesses. In their presence, we keep our feats to ourselves.

Still, our eyebrows were grown to raise. My retina to your retina, my nerve to your nerves. These cones are not occult.

Hundreds wore robes today, a redundancy of students in that same stage. Then scattered.

The grandmother misnames clouds as the Milky Way. Chicken tomato-blushed looks cardiac on your plate. I polish my own eyelids, knowing I cannot risk a touch of you tonight.

ver(bat)im

I am absorbent. I begin to feel your cadence in my throat. Expression.

I read a list of names from the diaphragm. Abecedarium to lung capacity. Inflect.

When I cut open the pomegranate, I am afraid it will stain my clothes, which I put very far away. The red seeds climb our bodies like ants until an ultimate swallow. Satisfaction.

Peel of exoskeleton. Your lizard eats crickets whole then sheds her skin under unnatural light. A little bit remains on the nose.

As I cut cubes of steak, I say meat is the best candy. You understand the Japanese men behind us, their plans not secret. My salad not undressed.

I twist to each spinach leaf. You respect fungi but will not eat them. You have only eaten venison in Slovenia in a park with deer. Let me. I will change that.

(trig)ger

Ninety-five miles away, my father shoots two bucks with one gesture. Venison for my mother's fifty-third.

Like the click of the cashier instead of the brutal silence of online shopping. Suggested for you, you might also like, because you bought.

Seven species of flower are in a bowl. I am no botanist, so I identify only four: carnation lily rose foxglove. The not quick yellow buds.

More water. You can drink from my strawless lidded.

Biology's letters. Alpha and omega of phloem and xylem. Vascular phone. Stems in water cell.

Then Dad gets a third deer for the night. Every mass has gravity. My body for other bodies too. Heliotropism.

But if I ate the sun, I would be embarrassed by the lack of blood. Iron want. Mars. Venus. Let them synthesize. Many plants agree with me, become carnivorous.

sp(ice)

Peppers, you claim, are delighted, burning. My check engine light comes on, sudden yellow.

You reject turmeric, saying it is bitter. But my favorite color.

I keep driving. Cinnamon is meant to be loved.

No thanks nutmeg, eggnog knock whose there. Cartoned. Cart on who. Yolk.

I tell you of eating raw garlic cloves. Anyone would do that because garlic has antibacterial properties. Anyone has a sore throat. It's a sinus the times.

Onion in onion on. Dish, please. Rolling highway tongue. They won't tell you it's veal. They won't tell you it's iamb. You never salt your meal, (io)dine.

Let me access your amylase. Pull-over halfway from picket pentameter. I become a neighbor without sugarless cups. I pocket jalapeno wine.

When you trace my perimeter with ice, it does nothing. Jarred salsa is in my corner.

cor(dial)

This restaurant once had communal knives chained to the tables. Would you like your brisket lean. I have to do something about this avocado. Halve.

Press my deltoid to administer me an ice cream cone. Grip my purse as I stand with fire.

Three sets of parents. One speaks of a hamster graveyard. Another of a teddy bear attacking during a ballet. The third of a doorstep dead rabbit on egghunt day.

People eating pie from wrappers. My tongue seems indecent with this scoop.

Someone can't let another win a race. She honks behind until he fingers the air. Backroad. Winds. A marquee's stomach mentions Dickens, the whole town potboiling.

We walk a black dog among deer that go to parking lots at midnight. That unknown and unknowing wild. Wraparound porch an ambition. We have home surrounded. Wave.

I go to you. Green dress with a knot. Cross my sleeves and dot my eyes.

Figure 2:

The necessity of time for sound

longhand

I think you live a different timeline. You add one month to each expanse.

Once upon: they asked him why he kept a knife in his back pocket. They didn't know what it was. On another continent, he was quite sure of his name.

Today, a comb handle still habits those jeans. I wonder at the effect on sitting. And they lived happily.

The hair is so important. Chests without opening. The mysteries are there, curling.

You braid my hair as I watch *Stargate*. Sand and sand and stand. So close and yet so alien pharaoh. I sit on you.

When you ask me if I want a real drink, you mean Old Country Time Lemonade. So far and yet so glucose. My thirst is purer, more ancient. The same as the one on each continent.

The Bile is the longest river in the liver system, leading to a delta of lipids. What's your favorite choler. Mine yellow.

The fruit shall set you free. I am a wedge holding adore. You like bananas in the fridge. They wait for your one mouth, your one tongue to consider cuneiform.

sidereal

What a bunch of phooey, Ptolemy. Copernicus was no Capricorn.
It's that same gravitational constant. Drop it—drop it now,
Galileo.

And how many modern mathematicians have seen the phases of
Venus. Closer to home, settle on mound.

Take off. Corn Belt or Orion's. Agriculture muddles the forest
and swamp. Get grains out from between my humid teeth.
Orthodontics to adjust oral space.

Eight morals or molars in my mouth. I will not recant, but tell of
when I saw Captain Kirk with Plato's stepchildren.

Air resistance is futile to fertile. Living to fall to mulch approval.
Flowers and followers to their beds.

The sheet won't hit the ceiling fan. You are no hypnic jerk. A
morning of eyelids waving across from each other.

When you enter the observatory, you are looking at the known
verse. You say lyrics long after the radio is out. My voice signs up.
Frequency makes memory.

Nostalgia is the unheard song of canthi, vertices of the eye, close to
but not vision.

(c)overt

You can stick-shift with a toothpick patrolling your mouth. Now prod a code in this door.

I am not impressed with the weight room. Light dumbbells and hunchback machines. But I am already strong enough to be your henchwoman at this rate.

I bear groceries up the stairs. You lug a cutting board, make chicken breasts into chunks. I spice.

A tactic: onions you cut yourself always make you cry. Slice on the counterintelligence. Raw baby carrots. Nutrition facts and ingredients lists are Steganography. Pass oregano.

Simmer cover honeypot me. I know there is a collection of Bond films in your drawer, but you've already forgotten the existence of the digital video discs. I can't reveal.

Surveil your online streaming of crime films. Weasel my way to pop, to pick that we see science fiction.

We form an alliance. We need to get smarter. Clean our dishes and black bag leftovers. Then touch until our fingerprints become a mosaic of norm.

hypnagoid

You dream you crash a party that aliens crash. Now tell me a NSFW story of Loki.

When we permute on the bed, earrings almost impale eyelids. This is a twilight zone world in which the people outside proselytize verbs. We go there.

Would you like something to drink. Do you need more time.

The tough questions are for nakedness at dusk. You once had sleep paralysis. You say my snag feels like I touch body to be sure it harbors here.

Fajitas please and I leave the beans in the shape of a slice of pie on the plate. Liverpool. Tell me about it. That architecture. Artery texture. You and brother in one photo.

On a sign we see Doctor G and the Mudcats. That's the spot. You give me such medical attention.

You desire a dirty comeback but don't grind your teeth. The wisdom ones are in sideways like periscopes against your cheek.

For years you didn't know how to whistle. Like a gene suddenly expressed, you made the sound of *The Good, the Bad and the Ugly*, a trinity out your lips.

Your blood, a low-pressure formation beside me, triggers my wake.

(24)

impen(ding)

You have I Can't Believe It's Not Butter in your fridge. Like it's still the 1990s. Fabio and the oil of vegetable.

I saw a DeLorean leaving your town. Forthcoming and going back.

College students migrate in. Congrats graduate out. Population scholar shipping. Glide the equator of semester.

We survive the equinox to startle the eve of an eve. Tempt the vesper in your ear. Sun of hot mouth, warm head. Your snuggle under the sum. Weekendings.

Smart assorted. The colors of an Uno game fill your closet. Fabric softener and Scattergories. I lose because I am an associative thinker.

Happy hew yearn. What is a yesterday but an accident out of range. Your point is as short as the day is longitude. I increase my lats.

(even)ing

Help me find the most scratchless frame. No wrestling matte today. I must have a Russell Edson poem behind glass. On the subject of myopia, dished as Petri.

We gain culture at the restaurant, Italian. Select menu. Adjust appetizers to disengage hunger. I choose a future of gluten-free pasta present.

At twelve you knew enough about computers. You did not fear Y2K. I did. I gathered coins like crumbs on an exercise mat and did one hundred sit-ups each Saturday.

As a child you touched objects an even number of times. The prime not sought, wearing sun divisor. Out of optic nerves, out of a mind.

Your skull is wider than mine. Your glasses refuse to hold my head, but I have more to shampoo. I, as adolescent, meditated that my vellus hair would fall. Moan of dark.

As a teenager on New Years, I let a Hershey's Kiss melt. These years, I only know it's midnight because of several sudden sounds.

We foil the evening with the odd, our leftover quips brighter than lasagna in the fridge. Cut through paused film of Bond. Refresh, lusted dirt of your olive for my glass-toothed cup.

un(hi)de

We look at images of taxidermies gone wrong. The pelt often remains the only truth.

Sometimes you are skittish with your wants. They spread like preserves on my grain-free preference.

Everyone has a right to fear. Aversion of the story. Instinct to have and make character, for glass and organic eyes to be thick with personality.

We may have a craving for the hybrid, but amalgams such as antlered, winged, or fanged hares are not fuel efficient. Phobia in the water. But lead with a baton of carrot.

When the greyhounds race, from my place I watch others bet. Ligaments of speed economy.

We are surrounded by hominids who think they are nice, and we love them when they are. How they feed us fresh, fresh peptides, pausing with hands.

canoidea

Sometimes I think my dopamine has crash-landed. Build a new empire while neuro burns. Violins is golden.

I equate a leaking burrito with a urinating Shar Pei pup. Both innocent. Folded, flatulent.

Storefronts list without commas. Juices Oatmeal. Tatt 2 Time, clock of cliché inks.

One of your clocks simulates a Chihuahua, tail pendulum. Trick tock.

Enough. Your gecko enters a plastic cave. A hawk scores the car of your mother's roof. Birds' next top taloned. Neither of us like hats. No real feather in it.

Un-conniptional shove improbable. Reason preferred. A logic of ferrets dwelling as obligate carnivores, their weasel war dance to pop music. Otter not happen.

Housebroken. But I did not like my potty set by the TV. Decades, and the deck's joined aces. Clubs. Go fish, but teach me how.

However many litters of mustelids, the world offers its badges. Pen one, and see how your trinket writes home.

rot(is)serie

If my curiosity is strong enough, that means I love you. I want to
know the paradigms that park in your lot. But reserved.

The cat that ate the can. At long last, haired expired. Who has a
final grin of metal.

Everything points to the ears. Cornless feet. Kneecap that cob.
Because I want you safe.

I enjoy flourless hours. Your kitchen becomes one big porcelain
bowl with a sink in the center. If you really want to know, I just
thought of buttering to taste.

Black water with sodium and sugar. Play catch. I throw it up and
you throw it back.

Finesse of delicatessen, I want a skirt of ham. Turkey blouse.
Roast brassiere.

I am a walking spit, turning. I kill two birds with one thrown.
Thus three are necessary. Let us share fowl moods, brooding shoes
that are like nests. Too padded. Release.

Feet and yards in a world of coal. Hot. I gather a new reddened
recipe, inspecting if you want to eat.

(a)ware

Who let the can out of the bag. Nobody but a hole. Let the cannot. Sever or serve airtight.

Bag in your arms again. How many times have you painted me. White lie, recline.

The line is significant in so many fields. I have crossed without holding hands.

I draw Dalmatians upon request when next to eggrolls. Sketch a frog on the yellow pad, its head low. The three-year-old adds a fly.

Somewhere the car is recorded as struck by lightning. Neither elastic nor inelastic collision. Nothing like how underwear grips. Night thickened with drops.

Water cycled like a tire. It slept and soaked like a spare. Meander puddles like a wet tightrope contest. Take the Romanians to a rodeo.

I put my hands behind my head. Your blue recliner is a truth. I surrender to your furniture and see what perspires.

langu(ish)

I can tell the paintings have been moved. Figure akimbo with squint and chickens.

They might put dirt in the urns. Just to see what happens when elbowed by company.

Sometimes I am not intimate with the English language that smells like cheese. But the taste lures.

The poet hooks a line. We will feast on decoys, hors d'oeuvres attractions populating toasts. The species pop up when done.

An ecosystem of bright orange barrels in the road to remind and ripen. CDs thinning in the backseat. I point to a list of song titles as form of transmission.

The center cannot fold. Our context is not origami ordering paper cranes and napkins for the sapid.

So many listen to radio instead of ratio. The restless and greater than signs do not lie but suggest a path. At the top of the charts, sounds with lyrics the size of ease.

An eraser huddles over a sunset, hesitant and luckily doing nothing as the fortune told.

leg(end)

Once I am lifted like Achilles from this neurochemical bath, I may be lost on a field.

I spend a day trying to remember German's *doch*. Knowing no-ing the no.

How your nose crinkles upon surprise, outrage, or joy is a good sign. Your organs loud. The length of a sound through memory roping.

My car is jumped. Startled and wired to not fright. Are you the right triangle, wholly merry. Go round. Teach this lessen.

We watch Canadian cultists sleeveless undershirted ski-masking with machetes in a forest chasing the coated. Hell is an unheckled film, map of cattleskull city. Character named Zap.

Too much marbling in this brisket. I cut a turkey into a puzzle for my stomach. Listen for my distrust of peanuts.

Press your pants into a sharpness. In your field, a podium blooms. Gait to it.

(sea)rch

Peace is thicker than unsweet tea. Potato salad is a soft gravel I put on a path of meat.

We calibrate. Your pulse within norms. I now pronounce. You refresh, a stasis in jeans.

Today, on the face of the world. Lightning slaps off the finger of giant Jesus ogling Rio.

Every statue is a sequestration. The season of sequins upon the carnal. Dance until a Wednesday.

Personally, Brazilian immigrant's outcome, I have momentum. Hips perpetual.

This state is easy to trace. Catharsis is overrated so I trap my mouth. Find pelt.

The microcatfish *candiru* finds inlets, not outlets. The body is subject. Urethra upturned.

Find piece, believe in the cod and prey heartily. You did not like seeing a goat cooked with its head attached. Think with the delicate. Lyrics are a musical delicacy you taste while driving to rest-stop.

(mime)sis

We watch men and women pretend it is the '70s. Call the appliance a science oven. Comb on over. Glad to not. My hair a long full falling.

We do not like nostalgia songs. Scan for other sounds. Funk of future in the road.

How many animals have stripes. A boot in the shape of a banana peel, parents surprised at a child's ripened taste for chamomile.

Tea earl grey pot calling leaves a message. An epistle of cups by the cabinet. I set these as a drastic measure of tasseography.

You allow your patio door agape for air. Flow of tree's crinkled enters. I would fear an envelope of cockroaches delivered.

My sandwich is instead a lettuce wrap. Icebergs melt in your mouth. Not in your change. Skill of an electric kettle. Keep your climate against me, free of charge.

corr(elation)

We investigate a long lost song I hear at Chipotle. On key, no kidney beans. Our happy find among lengths of fajita veggies remixing.

You do not do well with leftovers three weeks dead in the fridge. No one would.

I make grave decisions such as refusing key lime pie I brought for you. You tell me the scariest part of a film is when someone slips an envelope under the door.

I have not yet seen the family of raccoons. You mention with joy. Someone's parked car always has a stuffed panda in it.

I have recurring dreams of literally being a backseat driver. Endangerous. Duck.

Your prescription sunglasses have gone missing. If someone stole them, that someone has a new look.

Karma is a unique reptile. Our hands hold a diet of gentle crickets, waiting.

ap(pet)ence

While it is unlikely that bipeds would make it into the third-floor door you risk open, I would fear an animal infiltration. Six-legged especially. Youthful flies lift.

When I was nine, there was a praying mantis in the basement. The most fearsome among green exoskeletal carnivores. But he was calm as a monk.

Chirp and chirography. Letters or virtual games can spark the equation, but nothing like being close enough to brain waves.

The various ships between humans float, compile, cycle. This is a wet season. Monsoon or later.

The matrix of rain makes a calendar. The first quadrant of anyone's life had variables alternate. Non-ordinate. In abscissa.

Humor disorders the ordinary. A trashcan's stepper won't open the lid. Instead of crumbling small beasts into it, we usher their legs out. From under them. The properties of bellies are what lead us.

g(at)her

Of course the blood should have pressure. A peer walks into a lumbar, backs.

Every ten seconds, a child explains the meaning of sentience to parents.

We all have left a table without an excuse, finding our meals have skipped.

If we could only be the real animals we were meant to. I could be alone with the moss instead of worrying I may hit a biped on a skateboard.

How will butter change my life. The knife becomes slick. Always metal.

Some seeds are meant to pop, the thin arm of a root pointing to the other side of the world. Mini cosmopolitan.

Somewhere a handful of dirt walks and I want to forget. Add water. I remember this ecosphere is big.

Everyone has survived some apocalypse, no matter how small. Your toes and my toes are fortified, ready on the plank.

(gas)tro(nome)

I am no person of worship or favorites. Rituals of flavor, sure. I forget to write letters.

I would get out of the way of everybody if I could. Their tracks are spreading.

Across beds of blue threads. Prefer I be the big spoon, so stirring I am. I poke a thermostat to heat. Cover and wait.

I will never make you a sandwich. They are delivered. I make us better things. Not shrink-wrapped although many ingredients. I don't care how many calories are in this sentence.

Sprint to breakfast. Donuts are for driving. Become my passenger tracing arrows not meant for wheels.

Our steps will fossilize until the lagoon says differently. Meanwhile we are eaten by minutiae.

I forget my boots, leaving in other shoes with intentional holes. My skin gets air.

(h)eat

I lose my watch somewhere between "Some Like It Hot" and *Some Like It Hot*. Between Palmer and Lemmon, you are that second hand.

I am unusual today. I wear a black backless covered in hot pink corduroy jacket.

Let us speak of print making. Of the lessening for more. How an image requires a carve. Needs a knowing for what there is not or should not be.

And a placing of the paint, this method's tint and wink. Folds and press. Wet until dry. And we recur.

I take two blackberries in the gallery. Carrots could be eternal if it weren't for you, toothed. Even the crickets want those roots, though their sentience is the size of a twitch.

The results of someone's work are on the walls. Give them the eyes. Ears perpendicular wanderers.

Someone else says all paintings deteriorate. We don't want to admit. A deterioration is merely a change of clothes. Until the body is medium, mediating, meditative drag.

Transformation has a collar of time. Not on the wrist. Test the temperature of a new, raw milk.

(sp)rang

When I try to sprint today, both my quads constrict until instant stones. Heavy tight beneath my skin. Stop at my yell.

Pity the tongue of the sidewalk. Feet of taste, wear. Lace up. That is not your father in that car.

If there were a rat in your apartment, you would chase it. But sleep if you need to. Realize later to wash everything.

We, so pedestrian, survive the swerve of a van. Construction and walk signs. The green that yellows.

Your self-described game master style is chaotic. But I can control the enthalpy of your apartment. Feet outside the down.

Some are born with fine ears. Some have an office with windows. I enjoy believing they deserve. Some windows more realized than others. Life, not fare, but air-letting. We all lung for.

I help you tack up posters and call gray stickers magnets. A clear box of dice so you can teach chance. Crossed fingers agnostic.

What are the trances that you will sleep on your stomach.
Forget the half-finished chicken fried. Only the speed of memory at stake, waiting for the steam pots the eyelids shut.

c(lock)

I know where all the hot air goes. Let us spend an hour showing each other sillier and sillier videos of song.

The same jokes still work on you. Lucky, you are, fast-paced laugh innate choreography.

Clocks so loved the world that we are mortal. Reminding and rewinding.

And this renting of movies feels archaic. Aisles of horror films try to look me in the eye.

On a fresh afternoon, the harnessed puppy cannot chase the napkins. But licks ice cubes on the ground. Blue-eyed with pitter patter tongue.

We look at the world's current raptors. Outdoor chair perch. You say you love birds. The most loving person of animate and inanimate I know.

When buying crickets, we stop by cages of black-eyeballed wings. Each of their feathers a quivering story. Gray doves settle their heads. The shop will close in five minutes.

dis(posit)ion

We instinctively fear the crooked. But how many straight lines appear in nature.

I recommend eating the whole fruit. But they open those aluminum cylinders. It's crushing. What can the blood handle. Pots and pancreas.

Someone will have to clean. If we were in nature, the fungi would.

Emblems of owls across a room. Catchers of small, middle of a wiggle taken. Wisdom every twelve hours. Hunger stretching wing. Voracity veracity velocity.

Sometimes my stomach thinks it can fly. Steals away with legs of a buzz beast. I have an ear for it and find it.

Some mothers want me to eat and some are afraid I will get too big. Lived in a shoe.

I do not prefer fantasy. I like you in front of me, facing, the elbows' bends allowing possibility.

No natural predators but industry without civic or the ad hominem voice or daydream. Do not let me be one. Science, or something like it, may it fill the sky one day.

queue

Every once in a while, the crickets grow restless leg syndrome. I dream I hold a gecko to insects. Until gecko to gecko.

Tell me how populated I am. Most of my organs hypodermic. Test me, my cortisol not making the grade.

A train's metal recycling on a path. A regimen of vitamins, each rotation completes a new pie chart. Why are there no three-dimensional degrees. Oxymoron cart. It takes two to tangle, locate.

An infinite line can cover a sphere. Every group should have a token mathematician. You can hear the proof for why half of infinity cannot be differentiated from infinity.

Can help with your latitude problem. Geographer with two degrees. The ocean presents its species in a new league.

Double major in. See land whole. Sea lions are sea wolves in Portuguese.

Hunted to inclusion. Hinted to clue. Seal an envelope, that will make it across stationery sets of. Still, me.

whole(some)

I approach and you talk about compact numbers. If I am not good to you, tell me how I can be. Not goo. Tail me. I skid you not, I can acquire more properties.

One dyed foot attached to a keychain. Piecemeal taxidermies of luck. I had one and accepted it. Did you. We once were children but did not know each other.

Someone will build a fortune made out of the crumbs of each fortress. Between the heads of statement. A thought darts. Out of context, out of mind.

But enter a contest with shoes of inquiry. Up to a sleeveless judge. That way no need to roll. Pretty faces of dice.

Say cheese, the whole cheese, and nothing but the cheese. So help you mouth.

In the movie, a man shakes a complete Polaroid picture. Will something else. Appear.

And then apparent. A segment in reverse. Imagine if all those pieces of skin cells gathered and made us retrobeings. No, I am glad growth is an edit.

The same light never repeats itself, even if it has the same wave. Form and foam of you, me, and how far in a year.

pastimes

We look at photos of mixed. Pitsky. Schnoodle. Puggle. Horgi. Pugapoo. Cheagle. Golden Dachs. And all the vintage photos of dogs require a pipe in their mouth.

Need a light or more light. Or not as much, enough for proper shadows. Your pulled off socks stoic puppets. Vow of silence. I believe in other virtues.

Sometimes performing ventriloquy on silent films can be fun, as well as ignoring a classic through kissing.

List moments and possibilities. Do not number them, but shuffle them on a regular basis of seconds and thirds. Strike, depending on the sport. Pin a bat, bin a pat. Pitch to gutter.

I tell you I do want to bowl. Put three fingers. Most people learn in high school, maybe a field trip.

Have you ever accidentally used euphemisms. I mean, a real accident. I awkwardly patted the front of my ribcage when seeing an old friend. Drinking a cold, cold coffee.

(di)late

The way the binary system on a face changes, ring of iris smaller until hoop. Step right up. Leap right up. Greatest show you what I mean. On earth as it is in breadless.

Thyroid eyes have seen the glory. There have been times I have felt disappointed you did not read a book I left. I'd be crazy for reading about your paradigms.

Wanted alive. Warranted pacifically, silently, suckle. Nutrient density destiny.

Buy the large milkshake and leave it. There are better unbagged liquids.

Not drive-thru but drive up. Reverse with vivid lights, the shrink of the pupil, the left at the corner. Store my hands.

Overheard compartment. Defrost eavesdrop. Unfortunately, that outside light is replaced by your window.

For the rest of my life I will wake up at nine a.m. At the latest. I hear your water running, until face smoothed.

Erosion as it shall be, now and for. Every nimble nebula, galaxies sharpened. By humming.

(accele)ration

You have to understand. I'm still young and think success will slap me in the face. Nope, the pain is much slower, gentle increasing boil.

I just ate so much, I'm fuller than a Slinky coil. The inertia of an introvert is hard to graph. A week before I fall onto the next step. A weak.

When did they last perfume the road for mosquitoes. Their ambitions too simple.

Under construction, a hardhat is stubborn and refuses a ten gallon drink. You must know where spring breakfast. You put the bus in syllabus.

The wheels and the levers and the pulleys go. Fulcrum down. All through the town.

I'm interested in your technology. Screw. Ramp. Inclined science plane hammer time. Squared seconds with located mass.

Twist agriculture to pest your fertile. Redundancy of soil soiling itself. That is accomplishment. Life is how long your sentence is until you become a tautology, back to simple matters.

scope

Skill setting us. Down or up, society's web of feet. Are you sinking what I am sinking.

Fruit of the sooner or later, bite back to feed yourself. Treat your doggie paddle, rudder a rude tongue. Interview with a palate of Myers-Brigg types.

Earn your retrograde. Effort is not knowledge but only acknowledge, just as you need a climate to acclimate. Celery's nitrates and nitrites, nocturnal ritual snack.

If I were an exhibit, I'd break a legume. The dance is good for your health, but you lack a hall, so I am short on wallflowers.

Cannot live on infrared alone. Expectorate spectrum. Do you seed what I seed.

I, Taurus, straddle a Libra. Cymbals considered. Scales of a silent reptile that walks into water every two days.

Somewhere there are enough moons. Gong fishing. We will eat as loud as we want and live for it, our bodies sprinters.

reeling

Every time I close a window, you leave another open. The birds make it obvious, piling their chirps into bows. Err and arrow. I can find quiver.

The heart and other organ meats are worthwhile. Anatomy hill or restaurant. Or both. Crossed legs in the waiting area.

An online IQ test equates me with Da Vinci. My machines cannot fly. They begin to gather as words, validating the laugh of infinity.

My washing appliance has dissolved into theory. Trouble draining. I could stretch my clothes. Calculate an elasticity of sling shirt. Backyard lines we pin. The wind is full today.

The ocean is filled with lungs. Holes to a surface. Gas giants take their turn. Polite.

I hope you have enough bacteria. My system is literate, using colons and periods. Educate your tendons and pretend music if you have to. Drum nails with bare arms, your wrist a streamlined, trim mid-point.

Figure 3:

For a common center, shape

case

With all dew respected on this lawn of due processed, the deadline spins from a loom. A top, interrupted. Free screech on every screen. But I will not pay for cable.

Babble floats, pops. You are startled that I judge a fifth of canola oil improper.

I maneuver a joke into industrial lubricant too high in omega nine. For my taste.

Our nervous systems are complex enough. We can tell the difference between delayed onset muscle soreness and a strain. A hydra is not centrally nervous, rubbernecking our spasms.

Not everyone dances with their food. Glance with the depth of a deep tissue massage.

You are careless for the relaxing melody. Facedown cliché, back available.

Our first snow is graupel, hiving on cement, on each step of the stairs, leading to a room with thin blinds. Heat tugs my cold hands from sting.

foo(t)no(t)e

Do your research if eyes incite. A typewriter, being difficult, requires new feeding, and the decimal places itself second.

You wear pants that fit and standardized shoes. An ironing board with two left feet but keeping posture pauses for you.

New batteries for an old watch. Chips inserted into your delivered sandwich.

Many crunch by desktop. Old Floppy buried, squared. A box of crisps that imitate chickens in your car. Your heater, making a noise, accelerates exhale.

I can follow and drop you off. Mechanics see this happen all the time, and half the road is wearing cones. Orange for cosmetic purposes. Put the barrel before the fall.

Niagara gets what Niagara wants. My Brazilian grandmother zipped her coat and could not short-cut through Canada.

There is no problem with walking, with the alphabet the shoes spell in the dirt, a forward enclosed with licked attachment.

contin(gent)

Did plagiarism spread by mice highlighting. Perhaps we should use the word *epic* like the teenagers do.

Let's be elegant in the mathematical sense. If I had a nickel for every theorem, if I thought of a penny, if loafers became platform.

Some people are the children of poets. Some neighbor boys walk with a grape, asking if you want it.

We can calculate how much wisdom is needed to laugh or if snowflakes can melt into loops. Anything light can be lifted high. Few rubber balls are translucent with a plastic frog inside.

If friction were not possible, there would never be tadpoles. Much less could I say I am disinterested in newts.

And then we find that the projection screen is working. A landscape of thin light, bodies of glowsticks. A worm is not a glitch but a dweller. Every placard has a number. Half the time, it is odd and has a middle.

bildungsroman

Teach me how to say *Dedalus*. You and your waxed luck. Myths were your bedtime stories.

Labyrinth scared you, but I, at 20, laughed at a baby on inverted stairs. You became the kind of man who goes the long way down the ski slope.

A bump on the head is worth. The opposite of an Icarus. The signs told you what to do. You did. With Dublin in the summer.

The mind itself is a symptom. It builds, thinking *I can make it across Berlin on foot*. Or *study the English language in Austria*. Valid and possible, but thickly odd.

That is a beauty. Pareidolia puts its eyes on you and itches. Rubs like the best cat. If a cat were named after an herb.

Tell me of that chicken dish you can make. The one with frozen butter. An analogy was once sent to its room. Without dinner. Pacing until a new feeding began, the taste of sleep to full wake.

(app)ointment

I consistently reveal certain types of ignorance to you, such as how I have never seen *Predator*.

I worry that our lunch reservation is too late, that they will stop bringing the meat. That a *cafezinho* is supposed to enlarge my stamina into colors across a spectrum.

I think you will appreciate my asymmetric shirt. Working on my neutral-grip pull-ups. May I never fit into an old dress that had other assumptions.

Wait staff often tell clichés, and that is fine. Ask for the weight of the specials.

Yield sign up for my newsletter. Cross and comment when signaled.

Naturally, The Official Blues Brothers Revue gets snowed into Chicago because it's out of season. Who can put the fun in refund.

Yearly taxing, I no longer file my nails. Just clip. Beneath them is a gathering, an assembly, but I have a right to free, to clean. We could wait for an osmosis. Getting closer could help the process.

o(vers)ight

My bottled water's top falls out of my periphery. So the mouth remains uncovered.

During the play, you say the twins look nothing alike. Let us pretend that is a trick statement. One woman is playing both parts. Her expression the primary costume change.

Downtown with links of one-way streets. Turn right or wrong. The play also insists there can be birthmarks on the tongue.

You say babies look at you like you are insane. A baby in line for a burrito with pinpoint blue eyes. Precision is not the sane or same. As accuracy.

A virgin piña colada sweats on the table. I try to not be mushy. Can't change my striped shirt. I reveal I have a blender in storage.

I do not push buttons but un-. The moon is behind so many things. A dry, free champagne. The night with dichotomies. A glow or a shadow. Two cars switching into the same lane.

di(splay)

I want to call a rose the other red meat. All of the thorns removed except one. Tilted to me by myself through a pinch of the stem. Then to you.

We submit to paid parking. So many meters hooded by black plastic bags. Now bus lane.

Banners for mammals. Say the synonyms for behemoth. The museums become more historic each day.

Gift shops are believe-it-or-not's, that someone may want the solar-powered trinket. A breathless half-life-size plush horse waits at the entrance. I ask if you want a photo with it and somehow am serious.

The dying mall filled with chainmail equivalents. Putting on a storefront. Pull into a cold shoulder because the food court is so '90s.

Divert into the car. To coffee shop. I should not have drank the smoothie so rapidly. But I am pleased with how you interpret the curtains, pointing at the crinkled red signs.

(inter)val

Your brow holds leftovers from the chicken pox. A small scar. A pot grows mold at the bottom of the fridge. I peek each weekend, waiting for the changeable.

I remember when I soaked in oatmeal. My eyelids itched. Painted with pink calamine. Transformations decade before a millennium.

We sit in the second row. You do not like to tuck. In a shirt. Unbelted.

But dress shoes slacks. Lack it or not. An intermission is my opportunity to remain seated.

Coats with my lap. You encourage me to obtain vice. That is not my squeeze style.

Someone explains the plot to her parents. Many elderly in this audience, ready to laugh or become an extension of the farce. Coagulate into a new picture.

Washed for years, your jeans no longer quench you. Two slakes of a. Pair quick.

If zounds were secular, maybe I'd say it. My palms and feet so often cold, I have been taking the hormone of a pig to see what happens.

birr

Brazilians call a Sunday driver a barber. Barbers once bloodlet, so perhaps this is a comment on car injuries.

Toss me your red shirt. Still where it lands. Or I wear. See me inside.

How many accidents have you been in. Do you always know if something is an accident.

I think it is masculine because it is male pattern. Virility sea. Virility do.

Maybe my slang is antiquated, ancestral, tree-dwelling. But I neither climb nor swing.

Beard watching birds. A nest and nests. Net washed, ventured, gained. You prefer poultry, and I tell you I used to be like you. Now ready for steak stampede.

You are aware when you reverse. Try one direction and another. We migrate as a metal-cased unit, the sky another transfer possibility.

rebus

You once coated crickets in calcium. For your lizard. Now you choose an L-shaped option, a fake rock basin that fits in a corner. It's got the powder. When you remember to fill.

Set an adhesive-backed hook by a door. It can hold five pounds. Or a classy J-handled umbrella, pale wood finish. With a jacket, too.

Everyone cleans a cage while someone almost escapes from a shoebox. The Vs of front legs.

Syllabary on the ceiling. If texture texting with data plan or planted. The soil is relative, asking one question: have you grown.

Somewhere my piranha is dried and chipping. You, as teen, separating yourself from a gift of alligator foot on string.

What is alive has ticks. Jump at my sounds. Initially I will paint acronyms but not myself. There is and will be a machine for that. I live like I am my future, too.

v(as)cular

The perpendicular driver overlooks us, enters our lane with an inertial stamina. You calculate curves with the wheel and we make it.

I hardly braced in case. I am reminded how low my cortisol is. The heart is not a pound but an apothecary dispensing needs.

Pressure is a dotted line. Road or document. They will be adding a bike lane. Spoke and spoke. What if I wore a helmet in the convertible.

When a menu has mussels I am tempted. Your aphrodisiac is different, wobbly, with hot water in the process.

Twelve percent leg meat in the can of crab. You show me how to move the limbs of your ancient opener.

Drain, drain. A waiter calls you brother. My steak exists and is replaced with one most rare. Most people are not pleased unless there is blood in every organ.

peri(met)er

Sometimes I think I halve my cake and feed it two. Almond flour moon. Crave it crater and crater.

Up to no, good, and tide. Even in a parking lot there is a prime shine. We can find we hate the same songs.

I bubble questions for an hour until you are bored or because I thought you wanted a dance. Inevitable bundle of nay. Answers run out for the refrigerator.

When a door opens a light turns on. We park again on the same street. Slow service into the corner of the restaurant.

You rearrange your leopard gecko's environs. Cave, false leaves, basin pond permuted. She soundlessly scrapes the glass to learn new vertices. Becomes almost vertical against the glass.

Walls are made to be stroked. Your edges of genetic base, up to and beyond the armpit. Laugh until full, until body itself is a world.

victual

Someone suggests squirrels are in the back of the café. Not as food but preparing.

Your brother, when getting a food handler's license to dispense pickles, learned of anthrax and how to protect vittles.

Is privilege being able to have decorative logs in and out. I open a two-year-old packet of jerky. A small but thick white mold develops along the complimentary nuts.

How many hours can the food be left and still trusted. Into a baggie car trip.

Sometimes hunger is so deep it is a soft pain, perhaps the blood sugar too reduced.

Your hand low on my fat. No vegetable shortening. The meat kind or dairy tale endings.

You will sound like my mother if you question my habits. Let me treat you chicken cordon bleu. Can you imagine if blankets melted, how much we would need to shower when we wake. Either way we do, glisten.

cerebrate

Space is chaotic sometimes. Your dresser is in your closet. My watch, a simple fallen instrument, remains undiscovered.

The difference between an invention and a discovery is the birthing method. Is life a recycle, a has bin. Or knew enough materials.

You make tests for others. They handwrite, number, tinker, tailor, circle. Pass.

Print this on bright paper so my words are understood. Someone once ate the pi sign I drew.

Last name first, and the given made later. Nomenclature clutching at straws until found pen, word semi-permanent as needle. I have shifted, erased, shifted, augmented.

We are more than ten items or fewer. Shop or wait for gifts, bide for something good for the digestion. Some people's punctuation wears thin. We run on.

salu(brity)

The clerk asked where we were going. She took our passport photos. You with a haircut.

Someone told your father *your hair is speaking to me*. A scissor-based séance, science-less phrenology and some scalps more obvious than others.

You have memorized my birthmarks. I have told you my ribs are weird but you have other beliefs. And that, good, is.

If there were a Hippocratic oaf, his clumsiness would be benign. Reel in the sic, correct prognosis. We have no need to meet this being.

I am the kind of person who spits into a tube, mails it, and gets back biological data. All before the FDA can block the company's health risk assessments. My ancestry percents itself.

Continents, color-coded, wave to me. Make speculative print-outs, travel a font I like to reread.

eupepsia

You dry-swallow vitamins I give you. Everything comes down to humans teaching humans or wishing to. Washing down brain, unwanted. Assigned eating.

My eggs fail to enter one basket. They are polite and space themselves.

You are what you read. When we stood in line for barbecue all those months ago we saw a woman with a sleeve for her ponytail. Many things are wrapped for ease of feeding.

When you told me you did not like Joyce, I first thought, well that's that. But when other things unpeeled I could tell you were a bunch. More.

I do not know how punctual you want to be. I do not know when nausea leaves and cures.

Grapes sweat on cheese in the tray. Garnish a party of fingers. When the stomach is ready, sleep on it for two weeks to be sure the hunger is perfected.

(over)(ext)ension

We look at the rats in a Petsmart. They sleep. Quick increments of inflate and deflate.

Any animal with lungs balloons. What entertainer has done this, gas passing necessary.

You have picked me up, bringing me nearer to my car. All this time I have been sleeping in America for the past year, my car has been a few yards away.

Everyone finds an unexpected trigger in their pocket. A memory unconcealed that starts its feast.

I label mine and nod understanding. Then I open the jar. What is dispersed cannot eat me.

A wheel is not sideless, but the mere line of a circle is. A box of crickets kept until it is empty. The lizard eats what jumps before her, but sometimes she has to turn.

Air condition the amygdala, because my legs are as good as. Let the stimuli come.

We know a bridge when we see it, we know an overpass, and we are not afraid of lift. An elevator is the same set of doors, but it opens onto a new stability.

cyclor(am)a

Often you are that house. Lit on a rock. Or nest, crows'.
Steadying my home.

On the look, out. For me, always left-handed when meat is
involved, the knife.

If hands are a right, what is a privilege, that the desks are a given.
Only then did we have replicated problems to solve.

You read twice as fast as I do eat the contents of a bowl. I am the
fast eater, but when I read I tread into the holes of open letters.

I am living like the nomad who hasn't packed yet. Things set out
for animals.

Found art or drawn. If we blend the dichotomy with herbs, will it
work or play. Help my strained tea.

You can print this as a landscape. As a portrait. Escape with an
unauthorized use, machine's dried spitting. It speaks what we told
it to. We do not fear its office, its echo, its bellyful of blanks.

c(on)ta(in)er

A cricket holds onto the netted top of a terrarium. The heat lamp, the light lamp, the third wish that five insects will be eaten by the kept reptile.

You eat clam chowder only because you cannot tell what the creatures look like.

Your lagoon is served. Ask me again if I like seafood, if I am willing to watch them surface.

I have a procedure for salmon, experimenting on myself with a frozen piece expired two months. Secrets. Salt, an oven, and thyme. Passes.

I tell you again you are my favorite mammal. A normal American buying milk.

I tell you I voluntarily wore bibs until I was four. Hard plastic ones, one pink and another blue. Latch around the neck. Large lip jutting out that I would not fill.

My throat became too big for them. Your gecko will not eat crickets that are too small. And if something is too much. We can always get a box.

tem(porize)

We watch that movie in which a man eats fish out of an aquarium as a persuasion attempt. Reaching a bank.

Crossing. Water, arms in standard position. While driving, we talk about what if a car was named after Leif Eriksson.

Technique. You remember some sort of Celtic chess. Each rule and figures on board.

When you wake, each time you tell me. You dream that Tibetan monks play dodgeball in your home. You have not played in fifteen years.

At last man standing. A town creates the longest name. So it can attract.

Next, I learn the word *glamping* and do not do it. Baggage is as baggage does only if packed.

Your shower curtain is a metro map. Underground damp. If the door closes, you are moving. If the door is open, you are clean. But always winning my approach.

compendium

I am beginning to think that any plot is a MacGuffin. I read for sentences. Sin, syntax.

The mathematician's lobe of grammar. I ask one question in a shared foreign, and you respond in exponent. Articulate. Particular art.

Because of the anomaly on your bookshelf, I get to read Gertrude Stein's one crime novel.

Many exceptions nest within each other. One open mouth begins the process. Worming about until form, content. Will you be.

Graph, and the world graphs with you. Theorem, and you theorem a lone, long conditional needing treatment.

You critique my homeostasis, toes too cold. If a function had a body. If elegance had an expression. An equilibrium begins with the fingers, our oddities composing, rest of deriving leaning on my hair.

affix

There are word choices to be made. We will live through mysteries
we don't realize. Are there.

Is this a good place for any balcony. If someone makes it to the
third story. Listen. They would bring a hammer, you say.

Some regain drive after a refill. Pharmacist's mechanical reply.
Counter. Side causes effect. Just some herbs for my adrenals until
they have learned their lesson.

We cross the street with a box of Chinese checkers. If you had
a panacea, how long would it be in the oven. Can it be saved.
Fortune in the deep. Freeze.

I judge a good food by its facts. There's no tongue in cheeking fake.

Nutrient-dense intuition. Worth more than the sixth cent. Part lip
from lip then realign.

Economy of the body, its glycogen, its babble. Tell me that
someone designed a fat sphinx. A statue. If my anatomy is correct,
my eye-mask should work, and I will. Sleep within a bed of
minutes.

concoct

We do not choose the color and curtains of the room we are born in. Someone might as well let a screen door.

The hygienist picking and picking. So much of health begins with the mouth.

Slide the bacteria and find spirochete. Down periplasmic space. Whether prokaryote or professional.

The restaurant forks. Are only sharp enough to barely enter. Food pieces. Two elderly women in the parallel booth are signing.

With lemon my water needs more. When seven, I prophesized *I will write a book called Would Ducks Eat From You.* Nothing misspelled there.

Anseriformes or sans serif. Some birds kiss and others corkscrew. I said celebrate, not celibate.

Put your toothpaste. Behind the mirrored door. Care for your shelf. The duvet cover begins inside-out, but we know how to hold corners into possible.

megacosm

Fire ants appear in some bathrooms some of the time. Your lizard naps in her false cave.

I plan to exit a stasis because I haven't even been traveling through space. Chamber has its music and I have heard.

If I write of puppets the reader might think I mean metaphorical ones but I mean literal ones. That need puppeteers standing in view and sets on wheels. Can watch the human if you want.

You might not understand why there is a bear on the billboard. But that is its school of business.

If there is a door, you are on one side of it. If there is a roof, I might not always be under.

There are not always answers to the odd problems in the back of the book. Some problems are not problems but a possibility or a history. Parameter.

If you take your moment and share it with me, it can widen into. Digits growing. We can do more than count. On theory or in. No need to order, but a desire to, with take out.

Vanessa Couto Johnson's "Try the yen relish," a sixteen-page prose poem sequence, was released in a first BoxSet from Oxidant Engine in early 2018. *Softblow, Thrush, Field, Blackbird, Cheat River Review, Cream City Review,* and other journals have featured her poetry. Her third chapbook, *speech rinse,* won Slope Editions' 2016 Chapbook Contest; her second chapbook is *rotoscoping collage in Cork City* (dancing girl press, 2016); and her first chapbook, *Life of Francis,* won Gambling the Aisle's 2014 Chapbook Contest. A Brazilian born in Texas (dual citizen) and two-time Pushcart Prize nominee, she is currently a Lecturer at Texas State University, where she earned her MFA.